# Warwickshire

## Jean Patefield

First Published 2007
© Jean Patefield, 2007

All rights reserved. No reproduction
permitted without the prior permission
of the publisher:

COUNTRYSIDE BOOKS
3 Catherine Road
Newbury, Berkshire

To view our complete range of books,
please visit us at
www.countrysidebooks.co.uk

ISBN 978 1 84674 024 4

Photographs by the author
Cover picture shows Welford-on-Avon

Maps by Gelder Design & Mapping

Designed by Peter Davies, Nautilus Design
Produced through MRM Associates Ltd, Reading
Printed by Cambridge University Press

# Contents

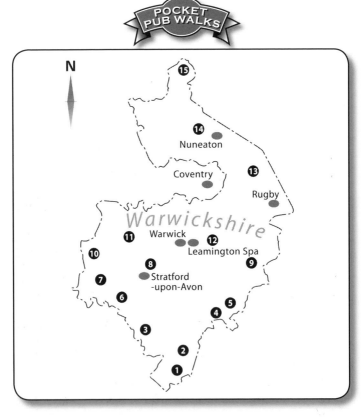

*Area map showing location of the walks*

# Introduction

**N**othing could be more quintessentially English than relaxing with a pint at a country pub set in a picturesque village and nowhere could be more appropriate than the county that sits at the Heart of England – Warwickshire. There are no seriously high hills or rugged terrain but there is much interesting walking in beautiful countryside and the abundance of excellent views will come as a surprise to those not familiar with the area.

The fifteen walks in this book are all between 2½ and 5½ miles long and should be well within the capacity of the average person, including those of mature years and families with children.

All the routes are on public rights of way or permissive paths and have been carefully checked but, of course, in the countryside things do change; a gate replaces a stile or a wood is extended. A sketch map illustrates each walk and they are all circular. An Ordnance Survey map is useful as well, especially for identifying the main features of views. The Explorer 1:25,000 (2½ inches to 1 mile) series are the best maps to use for walking. Sheets 191, 205, 206, 220, 221, 222, and 232 cover the walks in this book. The grid reference of the starting point and the appropriate maps are given for each walk

Warwickshire is famous as the place that gave birth and education to the greatest writer who ever lived. Shakespeare was familiar with many of the places visited in this book so you will be walking – and drinking – in the bard's footsteps. However, Warwickshire's history and interest spreads far beyond Shakespeare, enormous though that is. Most walks are complemented by the suggestion of a nearby place of interest you might like to visit to make a full and fascinating day out.

Nowadays pubs are often the best places to eat out in England and all the ones recommended in this book offer good food and a warm welcome. The opening times and telephone number of each pub are given.

The walks all start at the suggested pub. There is car parking in the vicinity and it often possible to use the pub car park. Do please remember to seek the landlord's permission first – always readily granted in my experience if you have already patronised his establishment or plan to do so later. However, it sometimes fits in better with the plans for the day to start and finish somewhere else, calling in at the pub part way round the route and so for walks where this is particularly appropriate, there are details of how to do this.

*Jean Patefield*

# Publisher's Note

We hope that you obtain considerable enjoyment from this book; great care has been taken in its preparation. However, changes of landlord and actual closures are sadly not uncommon. Likewise, although at the time of publication all routes followed public rights of way or permitted paths, diversion orders can be made and permissions withdrawn.

We cannot, of course, be held responsible for such diversion orders and any inaccuracies in the text which result from these or any other changes to the routes nor any damage which might result from walkers trespassing on private property. We are anxious though that all details covering the walks and pubs are kept up to date and would therefore welcome information from readers which would be relevant to future editions.

The simple sketch maps that accompany the walks in this book are based on notes made by the author whilst checking out the routes on the ground. However, for the benefit of a proper map, we do recommend that you purchase the relevant Ordnance Survey sheet covering your walk. The Ordnance Survey maps are widely available, especially through booksellers and local newsagents.

# 1 Long Compton

## *The Red Lion*

**T**his little gem of a walk explores part of the Warwickshire Cotswolds at the extreme southern tip of the county. It has outstanding scenery and views, as well as visiting the attractive village of Long Compton. Nestling in the valley beneath the ancient Rollright Stones (see Places of interest nearby), there has been a church here since the 5th century AD, when it was visited by St Augustine. Long Compton was notorious for its witches and an unfortunate old lady was murdered in the late 19th century because a local man thought she was a witch due to the toads in her garden. At the murderer's trial he claimed there were 16 other witches in the area. No trace of evil lingers over the village today, where the old blends harmoniously with the new and thatched cottages line the route that was once the main road from Stratford to Oxford. The walk climbs the hill on

**Distance** – 4 miles.

**OS Explorer** 191 Banbury, Bicester and Chipping Norton. GR 289322.

Mainly good tracks and paths but can be muddy after rain. One steady climb of 150 ft.

**Starting point:** The Red Lion, Long Compton. The pub has a large car park or, if you prefer, it should be possible to find a parking spot on the side roads in the village.

*How to get there Long Compton is on the A3400, 5 miles south of Shipston-on-Stour. The pub is at the south end of the village.*

the other side of the valley from the Rollright Stones and there are some excellent views on the not-too-challenging ascent. Your efforts are also rewarded by a lovely stretch of woodland walking, carpeted with bluebells and other flowers in spring.

**THE PUB** The **Red Lion** is an old coaching inn dating back to 1748. It welcomes walkers, children and dogs and there is a pleasant garden with play equipment to keep the youngsters amused. Indoors, there is a wood-burning fire, suffusing the ambience with the evocative aroma of wood smoke. The food is excellent. For a light lunch there is a selection of tasty sandwiches such as hand-carved ham on granary bread, or something from the starter menu such as spinach, gruyere and crème fraiche tart, or a bowl of soup with crusty bread is welcome on a cold day. There are also full meals available, including daily specials, the menu changing with the seasons. You might be tempted by the puddings, such as chocolate pavlova or amaretto crème brulee. The beers include Hooky bitter, Adnam's Broadside and a range of guest beers. Tea and coffee are served as well. At the turn of the 20th century the landlady was 'Aunt Phoebe', who not only ran the pub but also gave the land that is now the recreation ground to the village that she obviously loved, as her friendly spirit is said to still be present.

*Food is served between noon and 2.20 pm and from 6 pm Monday to Thursday and all day Friday, Saturday and Sunday, with a roast lunch on Sundays.*
☎ *01608 684221*

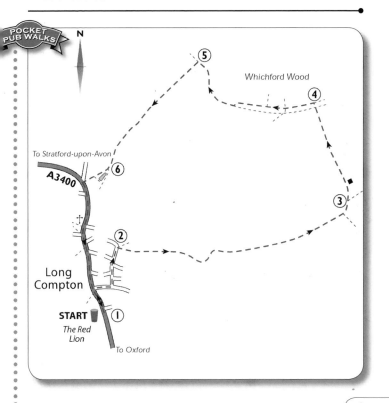

*The lych gate at Long Compton church.*

**1** From the **Red Lion** turn left along the main road for 175 yards, then turn right along **Butlers Lane**, pausing almost immediately to inspect the innovative modern sun dial on the right through a gap in the hedge. At the end of **Butlers Lane** turn left along **Back Lane**.

**2** When the road bends sharp left, turn right on a signed path along a track and follow the track for 1¼ miles to a fork.

**3** Bear left, uphill. Keep ahead, still uphill, at a barn on the right. At the top the track peters out but press on in the same direction, soon walking to the right of a hedge, to a wood.

**4** Go into **Whichford Wood** and turn left to walk just inside the trees. The path eventually comes to the edge of the wood. Turn right to continue in the same direction, now on a track. Follow the track as it heads downhill through the wood.

**5** Just as the track starts to rise, turn left on a clear track to carry on downhill, soon leaving the wood and with a view of **Long Compton church** below.

6 As the track approaches a pond, bear right on a path across a field to a metal field gate. If you find yourself walking with the pond on your right, you have missed the turn. Go ahead to the main road and turn left through the village, past the church, back to the **Red Lion**.

## Places of interest nearby

A couple of miles south of Long Compton, signed from the A3400, are the **Rollright Stones**. They are a collection of three separate groups: a circle of corroded, supposedly uncountable stones called the King's Men, a separate group of five a little distance away called the Whispering Knights and a large monolith across the road called the King's Stone. As is often the case, they are steeped in myth and legend encompassing everything from witchcraft and fairies to alien landing sites and ley lines. In fact, the stone circle dates from the Early Bronze Age, about 2,000 BC, and may have served as a calendar while the Whispering Knights are the remains of the burial chamber of a long-vanished Neolithic long-barrow.

The site is managed by a charitable trust and a vast amount of information is available on their website www.rollrightstones.co.uk. In a most innovative development they offer a guided tour as an MP3 download for your iPod or MP3 player. You can also download a modern retelling of the Rollright Legend. Don't worry if you haven't the technology. You can buy a CD with them on at the Warden's Hut and for a deposit they will lend you a CD player to listen to it whilst you are there. There is also an informative booklet available. The site is open all day for a modest fee and there is parking in lay-bys on the lane.

# 2 Exploring the Brailes

## *The Gate Inn*

**railes was once** one of the most important towns in Warwickshire after Warwick and Coventry. Situated at the northernmost tip of the Cotswolds, it grew rich on wool from the hills. The size of the 14th-century St George's church at the eastern end of Lower Brailes is testament to the community's wealth and ambition. With its imposing 120 ft high tower and the third heaviest ring of six bells in England, it is sometimes known as the 'Cathedral of the Feldon', *feldon* being an old word for an area of rich farmland. Today Brailes is a pair of villages that seem far away from the bustle of modern towns. Behind Upper Brailes is the still-impressive mound of Castle Hill. This is an

**Distance** – 4½ miles.

**OS Explorer** 191 Banbury, Bicester and Chipping Norton. GR 305398.

Easy walking on well-signed field paths. Lots of stiles. Optional climb to an excellent viewpoint.

**Starting point** The Gate, Upper Brailes.

*How to get there* Upper and Lower Brailes are on the B4035, Shipston-on-Stour to Banbury road. Upper Brailes is about 3 miles east of Shipston-on-Stour.

ancient earthwork and burial ground, later used by the Normans as the foundation for a castle. The route does not require you to climb Castle Hill but a diversion to the top can easily be included. It is strenuous but not very high at about 80 ft and is highly recommended for the terrific view. As well as exploring Upper and Lower Brailes the route takes in Sutton-under-Brailes, even quieter and clustered round an enormous village green with welcome seats.

**THE PUB**

Built of local stone, the **Gate Inn** is a fine old Hook Norton house, with a charming old-world atmosphere, including a reputed witch's shoe in the baker's oven in the lounge. There are tables set out in the lawned garden, which has an attractive view. If you can arrange it, the best day to do this walk is a Wednesday as this popular village local is famed for its fish and chips on Tuesday evening and Wednesday lunchtime and evening, with fish delivered fresh from Grimsby. The choice on the printed menu and specials board runs from sandwiches and light snacks to home-baked ham, eggs and chips, super pies and casseroles, local trout, breast of duck and lamb with orange and rosemary, with delights such as treacle sponge to finish. As well as the Hook Norton beers, guest ales are also kept. The local footpath group meet at the Gate so the pub welcomes walkers.

> *Food is served every session (noon until 2 pm and 6 pm to 9 pm) except Sunday evening, all day Monday (except Bank Holidays) and Tuesday lunchtime.*
> ☎ *01608 685212*

**1** With your back to the **Gate** turn right along the road for 100 yards. Opposite a phone box, turn right on **footpath 51**. Follow the path through allotments and across a field to a gate. Go through the gate and turn left to walk along the edge of the field to a stile on the left.

The route turns right here but it is well worth going over the stile and up the hill. The right of way skirts the base of the hill but the view from the summit is superb. Return to the stile.

**2** Turn right across the field to a lane. Cross the lane and continue in the same direction across two fields and along the right-hand side of a third to find a paved path known as the **99 Steps**. There is a plaque that explains its history. At the end of the paved path, cross a footbridge then bear right on **path 52e** towards the church. Turn right at a drive to the main road.

**3** Turn left for a few yards, then right on a fenced path next to the **George Hotel**. At a cross path carry on in the same direction, signed **'To Cow Lane, Whichford Mill, Cherington'**, to shortly reach a track. Cross the track and go over a stile into a field, then press on in the same direction along the right-hand side of this field and the next two, walking with **Sutton Brook** on the right, to another track.

**4** Turn left along the track to continue in the same direction. When the track bends left after 50 yards, keep ahead on a signed

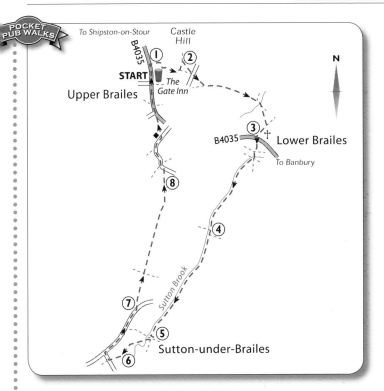

path. This shortly enters a golf course. The path is reasonably well signed across the course and essentially goes on in the same direction, staying roughly by the brook. Do not be misled when it crosses a ditch and ignore all paths to left and right.

5 At the end of the golf course go over a stile, some 50 yards uphill from the brook, giving onto a track. Go over a stile on the opposite side of the track and turn immediately right to a third stile and a plank bridge across a ditch. Go ahead to find a footbridge over **Sutton Brook**. Over the bridge the path is difficult to see on the ground at the time of writing, but lies

initially close to the brook and then bears right to a stile in the far corner of the field. Over this stile, walk across two small fields to emerge at the end of a track.

**6** Turn right to a road, then right again by the enormous village green. I think the seat donated by the Women's Institute is the most comfortable. At a T-junction turn right, signed '**Brailes** 1½', and walk out of the village.

**7** Some 225 yards after a speed limit derestriction sign look for a stile on the left. Go over this and follow a signed path half right. Follow this across several fields to a lane.

**8** Turn left and walk along the lane for about ¼ mile, ignoring paths to left and right. Turn left over a stile (**path 59**) next to a house called **Allandale** and follow the signed path through to the main road. Turn left and follow the road through **Upper Brailes** back to the **Gate**.

## Places of interest nearby

Many of the pubs visited in this book serve the award-winning beers from the local **Hook Norton Brewery** just over the border in Oxfordshire. It is one of the dwindling number of independent family-run breweries and is a fascinating example of a Victorian tower brewery still driven by steam. Founded in 1849 by a local farmer called John Harris, it is run today, five generations later, by his descendants. The Visitors Centre is housed in the original maltings. The shop and museum are open Monday to Friday, including Bank Holiday Mondays, between 8.30 am and 5 pm, plus Saturdays in December, and brewery tours are available Monday to Friday.
☎ 01608 730384

# 3 Ilmington

## *The Howard Arms*

**S**trictly **speaking,** Ilmington is not part of the Cotswolds escarpment but the scenery is very similar and the village deservedly lies within the Cotswolds Area of Outstanding Natural Beauty. Despite starting at the highest village in Warwickshire, the route climbs steeply to the top of the hills behind, the loftiest point in the county. These are crowned by a couple of radio masts that recall Ilmington's brief moment of national fame as the location of King George V's Christmas broadcast in 1934, relayed to the world from Ilmington Manor. It was introduced by a local shepherd, Walton Handy, who by all accounts stole the show, and featured bell ringing and carols from the village. Your efforts are well rewarded with outstanding views so a clear day is a must to get the best from this superb walk. It includes a feature unique in this book – a ridge path along the top of the hills with views on

**Distance** 4 miles.

**OS Explorer** 205 Stratford-upon-Avon and Evesham. GR 213437.

Field paths and a tiny lane, with one steady climb of about 250 ft.

**Starting point** The Howard Arms, Ilmington.

***How to get there*** *Ilmington is about 4 miles north-west of Shipston-on-Stour and is signed from the A429 and from the A3400.*

both sides. The return is exhilarating, allowing you to enjoy the scenery while striding out along a lane so tiny it has grass growing up the middle in parts and is provided with a seat to rest and enjoy the scenery. Ilmington is a most attractive village with a real sense of place, and is well worth exploring. It maintains the tradition of Morris dancing and some of the dances are specific to the village. The Ilmington Morris Men dance on several days throughout the year, including at dawn on May Day on Ilmington Down, visited on this walk, though perhaps not so early! Ilmington has a 12th-century church that is worth a visit and has hung on to its school, shop and pub.

**THE PUB** The **Howard Arms** overlooks the small village green and has won awards for its excellent food. The menus are varied and interesting and change weekly as they make extensive use of local seasonal produce. No sandwiches here, but there is an excellent choice from the starter menu for a light lunch. The puddings are incredibly tempting with, on my visit, for example, a delicious summer pudding with clotted cream or toffee meringue. The Howard Arms is a free house and serves a good choice of cask ales such as Marston's Pedigree, with guest beers that change regularly. With such a reputation it can, of course, be rather busy. As well as the traditional interior, there are tables on a pretty patio leading to the garden.

*Food is served every lunchtime until about 2 pm (2.30 pm Sunday), and every evening until 9 pm (8.30 pm Sunday).*
☎ *01608 682226*

1 From the **Howard Arms** turn right along **Middle Street**. This shortly becomes a surfaced path. At a T-junction turn right to the church. At the church turn left, then left again at the end of the churchyard to a road. Turn right for 100 yards. Take a lane on the left then bear right along **Frog Lane**. When this ends continue in the same direction on a path. Go through a metal kissing-gate and over a cross path and press on to a second similar gate and a footbridge across a boggy area. Keep on in the same direction to find a second footbridge.

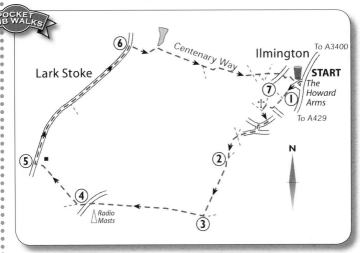

*The village of Ilmington nestles in the valley.*

2 Over the second footbridge turn left to climb steeply to a cross track at the top.

3 Turn right and walk along the track to a road, admiring the views on both sides and passing the radio masts.

4 Cross the road to a small gate some 20 yards to the left. Walk along the right-hand side of a field for 60 yards to a gate on the right. Go through the gate and follow the path, heading just to the left of a barn seen ahead, to find a gate onto a fenced path that leads to a gate onto a tiny lane.

5 Turn right and walk down the lane for just under a mile, enjoying the panoramic view spread out at your feet and ignoring a bridleway on the right.

**6** Turn right on a signed path along a drive. At an entrance gate go through a gate on its left and walk round the right-hand perimeter of a field. Before reaching a pond go through a gate on the right. Through the gate, go ahead, sticking close to a wire fence on the left, to a kissing-gate. Now press on ahead, ignoring a path on the right after 70 yards, to another kissing-gate and on through a third on the right after a further 45 yards. Continue across a field. Bear left in the next field to yet another kissing-gate. (**Note:** Not the stile in the far left corner or the gate near the far right corner.) Keep on in the same direction, passing the corner of the school playground and on across another field to find a wooden kissing-gate by a field gate on to a lane.

**7** Cross the lane and continue on a path signed, encouragingly, 'Public footpath to **Howard Arms**'. Turn left at the end of the first cottage on the left and follow the path to return to the **Howard Arms**.

## Places of interest nearby

**Hidcote Manor Gardens** are of great comfort and no small interest to the ordinary gardener with a small plot to care for. It is inspiring for us all to realise that this magnificent series of gardens was created in the 20th century from open, windswept Cotswold hillside. When its creator, Major Lawrence Johnson, came to Hidcote in 1905 there was only the manor house, one cedar tree and a clump of beeches. It is not one garden on a huge scale but a series of interlinked garden rooms separated by hedges. Johnson presented the garden to the National Trust in 1948, which still cares for it today. The excellent plan and guide is recommended to ensure you don't miss any bits! The gardens are just over the county border in Gloucestershire, 4 miles north-east of Chipping Campden and signed from the B4632. They are open every day except Thursday and Friday from the end of March until the end of October. ☎ *01386 438333*

# 4 Edgehill

## *The Castle Inn*

**T**he agenda for this short walk is views, views and more views. Of course, what makes good views are hills and this walk though short is quite strenuous. Perhaps it is an ideal excursion for a crisp winter day when, if anything, the views are even better. One of the vistas is across the battleground of the first major engagement of the Civil War. It is best seen from the garden of the Castle Inn, where there is a plaque explaining the course of the battle. On 23rd October 1642, the Parliamentary army commanded by Robert Devereaux, 3rd Earl of Essex, met the Royalist Army commanded by King Charles I at Edgehill. Thirty thousand Englishmen fought in the first major conflict of the English Civil War. The battle, which began in the late afternoon, was long and bloody and the following day neither side wished to resume the fighting. The King moved on to London whilst the Parliamentarians retired to Warwick. The actual site cannot be visited as it lies within a MoD ammunition facility. This route visits the ancient village of Ratley, which lies almost concealed in a fold in the hills. Most of the buildings are of locally quarried stone of a warm brown hue. The church of St Peter ad Vincula is worth a look and has an ancient preaching cross in the churchyard.

**THE PUB** The **Castle Inn**, also known as Radway Tower, must be one of the most unusual pubs in Warwickshire, if not in England. The Castle Inn stands on the summit of Edgehill. The octagonal tower was started in 1742 to commemorate the 100th anniversary of the Battle of Edgehill and was opened on 3rd September 1750, the anniversary of Oliver Cromwell's death.

Sanderson Miller, who lived in nearby Radway, built the tower. Miller made a name for himself as a 'gentleman architect' in the 18th century and had a hand in many fine Warwickshire buildings, including Warwick City Hall and Kineton church. The tower first became an inn in 1822, when a descendant

**Distance** – 2½ miles.

**OS Explorer** 206 Edge Hill and Fenny Compton. GR 373474.

Mainly woodland and field paths with several short ascents.

**Starting point** The Castle Inn, Edgehill.

***How to get there:*** *From the A422, Stratford-on-Avon to Banbury road, 7 miles east of its junction with the A429, take a minor road north, signed 'Edgehill 1 Ratley 1½' to the Castle on the left and the car park on the right. Note: this is **not** the road ½ mile further east opposite the entrance to Upton House.*

# Warwickshire

of Sanderson Miller sold it to become a free house. The story goes that he was a minister of religion and that the decision was unpopular with his family. Hook Norton Brewery acquired the Castle Inn in 1922. The building itself is interesting and unusual but the highlight is the view from the garden, stretching out across the battle site and several neighbouring counties to the Wrekin in Shropshire and the foothills of the Welsh mountains. Tables outside enable you to enjoy it with your refreshment on a fine day. As a Hook Norton house they serve all the usual beers. Unusual alternatives are the country fruit wines such as raspberry, or Old Rosie scrumpy cider. A wide choice of meals is available lunchtime and evening ranging from bar snacks and sandwiches to hot platters and steaks.

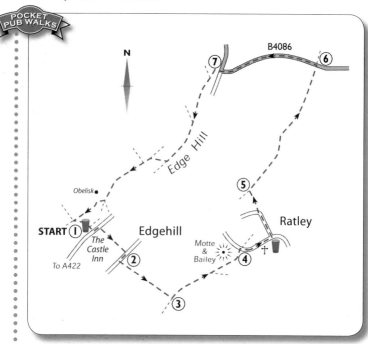

*Food is served between noon and 2 pm and from 6.30 pm.*
☎ *01295 670255*

*The ancient preaching cross in Ratley churchyard.*

1. From the car park of the **Castle Inn** turn right for 25 yards, then right again on a footpath just past **Cavalier Cottage**. Follow this through to a lane.

2. Turn right for 50 yards, then left on a signed path along a track.

3. At the end of the track turn left over a stile and head towards **Ratley**, seen ahead, to find a gate and stile in the bottom left-hand corner of the field. Once a castle towered over this peaceful village. If you look carefully just to the left of the village, you can see the remains of the mound or motte on which it stood. Over the stile, do not follow the obvious path ahead round the bottom of the hill. Instead, bear half left uphill, then walk with a hedge and wall on the left to a stone stile onto a track. Turn left to a lane.

4. Turn right along the lane. Note the carvings below the gutter of a building dated 1884, now a garage, on the right. Go past the church and turn left at a minute village green along **Chapel Lane**. When the road bends left, continue ahead on a signed

path up some steps leading to a stile. Carry on across a field towards a barn to find a stile onto a fenced path.

**5** Turn right to a metal kissing-gate and on in the same direction across a field. At the far side of the field, turn left to another metal kissing-gate. Through this, keep on in the same direction down into a dip and up the other side to a road.

**6** Turn left: a footway on the right starts after 100 yards or so.

**7** At a T-junction go ahead on a signed path. The start of this is not obvious at the time of writing. It is immediately to the left of a sign forbidding lorries to go left along the road. Follow the path through the woods to some steps on the right. Turn right down the steps and follow the path to a T-junction. Turn left for 20 yards. Do *not* go through a wooden kissing-gate but turn left to walk just inside the wood. Watch for an obelisk in the field on the right. Ignore two paths on the left at this point and stay on the waymarked **Centenary Way** just inside the wood to a cross-path. Turn left on a path with a handrail to help and follow this up to the **Castle Inn**.

## Places of interest nearby

On the A422 close to Edgehill is **Upton House**, a 17th-century mansion in the care of the National Trust. It has outstanding terraced gardens that are a delight to explore and the restaurant serves the usual excellent lunches and teas that we expect from the National Trust. The contents of the house include an interesting exhibition of Shell advertising posters and an Art Deco bathroom with a dramatic colour scheme of red, black and silver. It is open every afternoon from mid March until mid December.
☎ *01295 670266*

**The Dassetts**

*The Avon*

**W**arwickshire doesn't have any wild country and the Burton Dassett hills are about as close as it gets. They are a range of low, bare hills jutting out of the surrounding plain. This means there are tremendous views in all directions and the climb to the top is well rewarded. The hills have intriguing bumps and hollows. These are the legacy of quarries where the warm brown stone used extensively in the surrounding villages was quarried. This route also explores four villages clustered round the base of the hills. One, Burton Dassett, has a fascinating ancient church that is well worth a look and Avon Dassett boasts an excellent pub.

This is quite a long and hilly walk that makes a good all-day expedition. If you wish to break the walk at the pub for lunch a good plan is to start at the car park at Burton Dassett country park (charge), which is well signed in the area, and pick up the route at point 7.

**THE PUB** Originally built in the 18th century, the **Avon** in Avon Dassett is a delightful traditional country pub complete with wood floors, beams and a blazing open fire in winter. In summer, there are tables outside shaded by trees and parasols. At times in its long history it has also been known as the **Prince Rupert**. A free house, they keep Hook Norton bitter, Courage Directors and Theakston's. The extensive menu ranges from doorstopper sandwiches to full meals. The enterprising centrepiece is 64 ways to enjoy sausage and mash, featuring any combination of four types of sausage, four varieties of mash and four flavours of gravy. There are also some wickedly tempting puds, including a sinful chocolate fondue: perhaps not for you if you still have some of the walk to do!

*Food is served from noon to 2.30 pm in the week and later at the weekend, and every evening except Sunday.*
☎ *01295 690270*

**Distance** 5½ miles.

**OS Explorer** 206 Edge Hill and Fenny Compton. GR 409499.

Field paths connecting attractive villages in undulating terrain, with one sharp climb.

**Starting point** The Avon in Avon Dassett.

**How to get there** *Avon Dassett is signed from the B4100, Gaydon to Banbury road. The Avon pub is on the main road through the village at the west end.*

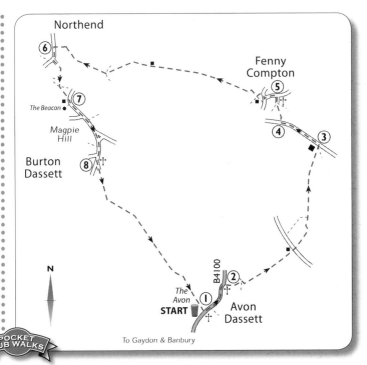

Northend
Fenny
Compton
The Beacon
Magpie
Hill
Burton
Dassett
N
The
Avon
START
Avon
Dassett
B4100
To Gaydon & Banbury

POCKET
PUB WALKS

1. With your back to the **Avon**, turn left and walk up through the village, passing **St Joseph's church** on the right, as far as **St John the Baptist church**, also on the right.

2. At the far side of the churchyard, turn right on a signed path and follow it to a drive. Turn right for a few paces then left over a stile. Walk along the left-hand side of a field to a field gate, along a short stretch of fenced path, and then across a field to emerge on a lane just to the right of a house. Cross the lane and continue on a permissive path across a field. Follow the path as it bears left and joins the right of way. Press on in the same direction to come out on a lane 100 yards to the right of a large modern barn.

3 Turn left for just over ¼ mile.

4 Opposite **The Grange** turn right on a signed path to walk across a field towards a church, to a tiny lane in **Fenny Compton**. Turn right. At a road turn left. At a T-junction turn right along **Bridge Street** for 30 yards.

5 As the road bends right, continue along a track to **Wood Barn**. At the

*A climb up to the beacon is well worth it for the superb view.*

entrance to **Wood Barn** turn left, then turn right on a cross path in front of a modern barn. Follow the waymarked path in a more or less straight line across several fields, navigating from stile to stile, to a stile by a field gate about 200 yards after passing a barn. Now bear slightly left to a kissing-gate by a field gate, crossing a track at the far side of the field. Press on over the shoulder of the hill, initially along the right-hand side of a field and then on in the same direction when the fence veers right. Through a kissing-gate, bear right to another gate onto a track and follow this into **Northend**.

6 Turn left along a road, then left again along the first lane, immediately before **Stone Cottage**. Continue ahead when this shortly ends at a metal field gate, going over three stiles. Now follow the path slightly right to a fourth stile and on in the same direction, steeply uphill, to a car park and picnic site below **The Beacon**, a round stone structure on one of the humps. It is well worth climbing a little further up to it for the superb view before resuming the route.

**7** Walk along the drive from the car park to a T-junction at the entrance kiosk. Turn left to continue in the same direction, climbing **Magpie Hill** on the right for another view, if you wish. Bear right at a fork, signed **'Burton Dassett Church'**. Bear left at the next fork and left again after a few yards to the church.

It is well worth taking the time to visit this ancient church. There has been a place of worship on the site since at least 1087 but much of the present structure dates from the 13th century, when it lay at the centre of a thriving market town! It has interesting medieval wall paintings and stone carvings and there is information on its history and points of interest within.

**8** Follow the path to the right of the church, signed **'Avon Dassett 1¼ miles'**, to leave the churchyard at a gated stile. The path is now easy to follow along the foot of the hills on the left, walking from stile to stile, to eventually find a metal field gate giving on to a short track that emerges in **Avon Dassett**, next to the pub.

## Places of interest nearby

The **Heritage Motor Centre** at Gaydon on the B4100 is heaven for the car enthusiast. There are more than 150 cars on display representing 100 years of motor manufacture in Britain from the many companies that have been part of the industry, some of whom are still in business whilst others have long since disappeared. There is not just a great array of cars to see, but many other items from Britain's motoring heritage. For example, Lord Nuffield's office, carefully recreated with all the original artefacts from his Oxford factory, sets out the modest work place of one of the most influential men in the motor industry – William Morris, of Morris/MG. The Centre is open every day except Christmas, between 10 am and 5 pm.
☎ *01926 641188*

# 6 Welford-on-Avon

## *The Bell Inn*

**W**elford-on-Avon lies in a major bend on the River Avon and so is surrounded by water on three sides. It has won Warwickshire's best-kept village competition several times. This takes no account of how inherently attractive a place is but judges the civic pride the inhabitants show by the care with which they maintain it. Nonetheless, Welford is a charming village, with a wealth of ancient thatched cottages. On the village green there is a tall maypole, now made of aluminium, and the latest to have stood there in a tradition dating back to the 14th century. This easy stroll uses paths and lanes that weave between the cottages and also includes two different stretches beside the Avon and a visit to the neighbouring hamlet of Weston-on-Avon. It is ideal to walk off an excellent lunch or sharpen the appetite for dinner at the famous Bell Inn.

**Distance** - 3 miles.

**OS Explorer** 205 Stratford-upon-Avon and Evesham. GR 148522.

Village footpaths and lanes, field and riverside paths.

**Starting point** The Bell Inn, Welford-on-Avon.

***How to get there*** *Welford-on-Avon is signed from the B439, Stratford-upon-Avon to Bidford-on-Avon road. The Bell Inn is on the right as you enter the village.*

**THE PUB** The **Bell Inn** in the centre of Welford-on-Avon has been well known for its food for a long time. According to local tradition, Shakespeare was on his way home after meeting Drayton and Ben Jonson for a drink at the Bell when he contracted fatal pneumonia from getting wet through. Thirty odd years ago it was famous for its chicken curry at a time when the best you could hope for in most pubs was a dusty pork pie or perhaps a pickled egg. We always imagined that they doled the curry out from huge vats to the enthusiastic hordes. It is now very smart (see the washbasins in the loos!) but they have been successful in maintaining the welcoming cosy village pub ambience in the bar with an open fire. The quote from Orson Welles on the glass round the wine store struck a particular chord with me.

The interesting menu does not neglect the old favourites. For a lighter meal at lunchtime there are sandwiches and a ploughman's lunch served with a selection of interesting cheeses, or you could try something from the starter menu such as, for example, deep fried brie with apricot and ginger compote. The beers include Hooky bitter and Wadworth 6X. There is a stylish garden to enjoy in the warmer weather.

*Food is served every lunchtime until about 2.15 pm and in the evening.* ☎ *01789 750353*

**1** From the **Bell Inn**, go right along **High Street** for 30 yards. Turn left on a path signed **'Avon Valley Way'**. Continue in the same direction when it becomes a surfaced drive, to reach a lane.

**2** Turn left, admiring the superb thatched house, on the left. The lane ends at **Pear Tree Close**. Carry on in the same direction above the **River Avon** (if it is muddy there is a permissive path to the right) to a lane in **Weston-on-Avon**.

**3** Cross the lane and go on in the same direction along a track. When the hedge on the right ends, follow the track round to the right past some cottages. Continue on the track as it then bends left, becomes a

*The maypole on the village green in Welford-on-Avon.*

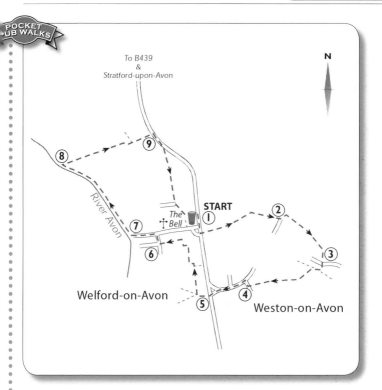

POCKET PUB WALKS

To B439
&
Stratford-upon-Avon

N

⑧ ⑨

River Avon

⑦ START
The ① ②
✝ Bell

⑥ ③

Welford-on-Avon ④

⑤ Weston-on-Avon

path and then a drive. Shortly the path lies to the left of the drive, separated by a hedge, and then ends at a lane.

④ Turn right to a T-junction after a few yards. Turn left and walk up to a T-junction with the main road through **Welford-on-Avon**. On the right is the village green with its maypole, round which the local children dance every July.

⑤ Cross the road and turn left for a few yards to a surfaced path starting through a metal kissing-gate. After 100 yards, at the end of a hedge on the right, turn right on a waymarked path that leads behind cottages. Ignore a waymarked path on the right and stay on the path ahead as it zig-zags down to a lane.

6 Turn right to the church, then left down **Boat Lane** past some of the prettiest cottages in the village. At the end of **Boat Lane** take a path bearing right to the **River Avon**.

7 Turn right beside the river on a permissive path, walking from one small metal gate to the next.

8 At the end of the third field, when the way ahead is through a metal field gate, turn right and walk along the left-hand side of a field. Go through a gate on the right onto a playing field and ahead a few yards to a gate onto a track leading to a road,

9 Turn right along the footway for 125 yards, then bear right on a signed path. Cross the end of a lane and bear left on a path that ends at a tall kissing-gate. Go ahead along a drive for 30 yards, then turn left up steps to emerge next to the **Bell**.

## Places of interest nearby

Welford-on-Avon is just south-west of **Stratford-upon-Avon** where there are numerous places of interest connected with Shakespeare. If you feel like a change from bard-related activities, however, something a bit different is **Stratford-upon-Avon Butterfly Farm** located on the south bank of the Avon in Swan's Nest Lane. Here you can watch exotic butterflies fly and feed as well as seeing their life cycle in action. Some other interesting insects are kept here, too, such as stick insects and leaf-cutting ants. They are open every day except over Christmas from 10 am until 6 pm in summer and until dusk in winter.
☎ 01789 415878

# 7 Wixford & Exhall

## *The Three Horseshoes*

**M**id-Warwickshire has some of the county's prettiest villages, with many thatched cottages that could grace the lid of any chocolate box. One of these is Exhall, reputedly one of the villages visited by Shakespeare on drinking trips with his friends. Today it has no pub so this route is based round the unusually attractive hostelry in the neighbouring scattered village of Wixford. After a saunter along the lane to and through Exhall, a track and a field path lead to a wood crowning the highest hill in these parts. The route skirts the hill rather than climbing it, as a wooded hill has poor views. The wood has many deciduous trees that are particularly colourful in autumn. The return, however, has some excellent vistas down the Vale of Evesham to the Cotswolds beyond.

**Distance** - 4 miles.

**OS Explorer** 205 Stratford-upon-Avon and Evesham. GR 092544.

Mainly good tracks and lanes.

**Starting point** The Three Horseshoes, Wixford.

***How to get there*** *Wixford is just east of the A46. From the junction of the A422 and A435 at a roundabout just south-west of Alcester, follow the signs to Wixford, starting along the A422 towards Worcester before shortly taking a signed minor road to Wixford and the Three Horseshoes on the right.*

**THE PUB**

The **Three Horseshoes** is an exceptionally attractive country pub, with an outstanding flower-filled patio behind, that has tables beneath a shady pergola. The lunch menu features substantial sandwiches served with salad and crisps or filled jacket potatoes. For heartier appetites there is a choice of sausage and mash or fish, chips and mushy peas and the full à la carte menu is also available at lunchtime. On Sundays full roast lunch is served instead of the lighter lunch menu offered the rest of the week. The beers include Marston's Pedigree, Adnams and Timothy Taylor. The building dates back to at least the early days of the 19th century and has been a smithy at one time. The spirit of the blacksmith is said still to be present ...

*Food is available between 12 noon and 2 pm and from 6.30 pm onwards*
☎ *01789 490400*

1️⃣ Take the lane opposite the **Three Horseshoes**, signed **'Exhall**

**village ¾ Arden Grafton 1¾ Temple Grafton 2½'**, for 100 yards, then turn left, signed **'Exhall village only'**. Walk along the lane into and through **Exhall**, ignoring all signed paths to left and right.

**2** Shortly after a pronounced right-hand bend, turn left on a signed bridleway, waymarked as the **Arden Way**, starting through the farmyard of **Valley Farm**. At the end of the farmyard keep on in the same direction along a track until the track ends at two gates. Go through the gate on the left to maintain direction, now on the right-hand side of a field, to a small metal gate at the far end of the field.

**3** Through the gate turn left immediately on a small, unsigned path just inside the wood. Carry on in the same direction as a path

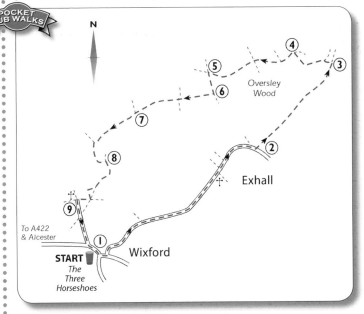

*Oversley Castle is glimpsed through the trees near point 6.*

shortly joins on the right, soon passing a metal hide on a tree on the left. The path is narrow but clear and remains just inside the wood until it swings away from the edge to shortly meet a broad track.

4 Turn left for ½ mile and ignore all side paths.

5 Watch for a cross-path where the left path is larger than that to the right. (This is the second obvious cross-path.) Turn left and follow the path towards the edge of the wood.

6 Turn right. At the end of the wood carry on in the same direction

along a hedged path to a T-junction with a track.

**7** Turn left. At the next track junction, turn left again to a T-junction with a drive.

**8** Turn right to a tiny lane, little more than a surfaced track. Just to the right at the junction with the lane, almost hidden by ancient yews, is Wixford's church (see *Places of interest nearby*).

**9** Turn left and this leads back to the **Three Horseshoes**.

## Places of interest nearby

**Wixford church** contains some fine 15th-century brasses. The church is often locked but the key is available locally. It is dedicated, unusually, to St Milburga. She was the daughter of a local chieftain in the Shropshire area and became abbess of a convent founded by her father. As well as being well connected she was apparently also beautiful and had the usual trouble fighting off rapacious suitors. The thatched wooden shed in the churchyard was built as the stable for the horses of visiting clergy.

**Alcester** is 2 miles north of Wixford. It is well worth a wander round and many of its ancient buildings have been carefully renovated. Malt Mill Lane, in particular, is lined with magnificent rows of medieval timber-framed houses with projecting upper storeys. It lies on Ryknild Street, the great Roman road that ran from Wall near Lichfield to Stow-on-the-Wold, and there have been many finds from that era. They are housed in an excellent museum on Priory Road that combines well-displayed artefacts with interactive features to bring the Roman town vividly to life. It is open Friday and Saturday between 10 am and 4 pm and on Sunday between 2 pm and 4 pm.
☎ *01789 762216*

# The Foxhunter

**I**n a few short miles the varying uses of this undulating countryside are demonstrated by this walk as it traverses a golf course, a nature reserve and a working fruit farm. The golf course is highly manicured, of course, but it is hard to object when it has been heavily planted with native trees, which will become more magnificent as the years roll by. The nature reserve is managed for conservation and is lightly grazed to encourage species diversity. As you cover the outward leg of the route from Snitterfield the views get better and better, to reach a climax at an obelisk overlooking Stratford-upon-Avon. You can see as far as Edgehill (see walk 4), the Cotswolds and the Malverns and there is

**Distance** - 4 miles.

**OS Explorer** 205 Stratford-upon-Avon and Evesham. GR 213598.

A very varied route through farmland, golf course and nature reserve.

**Starting point** The Foxhunter pub in Snitterfield.

*How to get there* *Snitterfield is about 4 miles north of Stratford-upon-Avon and is signed from the A46.*

a viewfinder to help you work it all out. A clear day is a must.

You would think that such a magnificent obelisk must commemorate a great battle or other turning point in our country's history. Not so! It was erected in memory of one Robert Needham Phillips, who was MP for Bury in Lancashire for 22 years and came to live in this area. The return leg crosses more of the golf course and then a working fruit farm. This could perhaps be called scruffy by comparison with the earlier stages of the walk but this is countryside for production rather than show. The blossom is lovely in season and it is a hive of activity at harvest time.

**THE PUB** The **Foxhunter** in Snitterfield is a friendly village pub that serves Bombardier, Worthington's, various guest beers and Snipe. This latter is brewed in the village with a donation from each pint going to village causes through the Parish Council. The lunch menu includes sandwiches served with salad or chips, soup and a selection of homely and tasty specials such as cottage pie or fish and chips. There is a much more extensive evening menu served Tuesday to Saturday. The Foxhunter has an attractive and cosy atmosphere inside and there are some tables outside overlooking the village square.

# Warwickshire

*Food is served from 12 noon to 2 pm, and Tuesday to Saturday evenings from 7 pm to 9 pm.*
☎ *01789 731224*

**1** Turn left out of the **Foxhunter** and follow the road up through the village towards the A46. At the edge of the village, next to the **White Horse House**, turn right on a signed path. This leads into a field. Turn left across the field to a kissing-gate onto a road.

**2** Turn right to shortly cross a bridge over the **A46**. Ignore a road on the right and stride out for a good ½ mile.

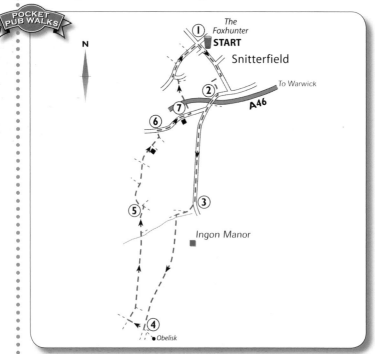

[3] Just before a pronounced left-hand bend in a dip, turn right on a signed path. When the fence on the right ends, stay close to the hedge on the left to find a stiled footbridge leading onto **Ingon Manor golf course**. Turn left over this. The path now goes ahead, initially between newly-planted trees, heading for an **obelisk** seen ahead. At the time of writing, the path is not well signed, with just an occasional arrow on a post. Head for the **obelisk**. As you get closer you can see that it appears to be surrounded by woods. Now head for the right-hand side of the wood to find a kissing-gate off the golf course into Welcombe Hills Country Park and nature reserve. This is about 50 yards to the right of the edge of the wood. Go ahead to a clear cross-path.

*The memorial to Robert Needham Phillips, MP.*

[4] To continue with the route, turn right. However, for the best views, it is well worth going a short distance left to the **obelisk**, then returning to this point and continuing along the path to a metal field gate. Do not go through the gate but turn right along the left-hand side of the field. At the end of the field go through a wooden kissing-gate to continue in the same direction beside a newly planted wood. Keep going in the same direction across a field and more of the golf course to eventually reach three small bridges over a stream. Go over the one on the right, through a gap in a hedge and on, still in more or less the same direction, across more fields to find a cross-track near some glasshouses.

**5** Turn left along the track. When the track turns right at a barn on the right, keep ahead to a drive. Turn left along the drive to a road.

**6** Turn right for about ¼ mile.

**7** Some 50 yards after **Shakespeare's View** go through a kissing-gate on the left. Go straight across an orchard to a kissing-gate and steps onto the **A46**. Choose your moment to cross this busy road, then keep on along a path in the same direction to join a drive leading shortly to a lane. Turn left to a T-junction, then turn right through **Snitterfield** back to the start.

## Places of interest nearby

**Warwick**, 5 miles north-east of Snitterfield, has many buildings of historic interest including, of course, the dramatic medieval castle, home to generations of influential Earls of Warwick. This has many fascinating displays but perhaps deserves a whole day to enjoy what it has to offer. Equally interesting but on a smaller scale is the **Lord Leycester Hospital**, which is an historic group of 14th-century buildings clustered round the Norman gate at the west end of the High Street. For 150 years it was home to Warwick's medieval guilds. In the reign of Queen Elizabeth I, it became a hospital and retirement home for old soldiers and so it remains today as a self-supporting charity. Those who live there are called the Bretheren and they used to be provided with food and drink from the Bretheren's Kitchen. Today, this serves light lunches and refreshments to the public between Easter and October. Also open in summer is the small but delightful **Master's Garden**. The buildings themselves are open all year, every day except Monday (open Bank Holidays) from 10 am until 4 pm in winter and 5 pm in summer.
☎ *01926 491422*

# 9 The Grand Union Canal

## *The King's Head*

**The two parts of this walk** could not be in greater contrast. The first stretch is by the Oxford and the Grand Union canals near their junction, so is level walking by the mainly peaceful waterway fringed with wild flowers in season. There is also the interest of watching the boats chug by, especially entertaining on a summer Saturday when the novices pick up their hire boats at the marina and have to navigate their way out at the canal junction. The route then leaves the canal and climbs through the beautiful parkland of the Shuckburgh estate to the summit of Beacon Hill. The views from the top are well worth the effort and are spread out at your feet as you descend back to the King's Head pub at Napton.

The **King's Head** on the edge of Napton-on-the-Hill has been a pub since it was built over a hundred years ago and draws trade from both the village and the nearby canal. It is a Hook Norton house and keeps their full range of beers. At lunchtime the bar menu features a range of sandwiches, including a tasty sausage and onion, or filled jacket potatoes. A full evening menu is also available and this changes regularly. On my visit I enjoyed baked cod with a horseradish and herb crust on spinach mash. The puddings are excellent and include such treats as a baked cheesecake. There are some tables outside.

*Food is served between 12 noon and 2 pm and from 6 pm onwards.*
☎ *01926 812202*

1 From the **King's Head**, cross the main road and walk along **Tomlow Lane** to a bridge over the **Oxford Canal**. Go down to the towpath and turn left by the canal. At a canal junction go over the bridge and carry on in the same direction as far as **footbridge number 105**.

*As far as the canal junction the path lies beside the Oxford Canal,*

**Distance -** 5 miles.

**OS Explorer** 222 Rugby and Daventry. GR 465618.

Canal towpath and well signed paths across estate fields and parkland, climbing steadily to viewpoint at summit.

**Starting point** The King's Head, Napton.

**How to get there** *The King's Head is on the A425, about 3 miles east of Southam on the outskirts of Napton.*

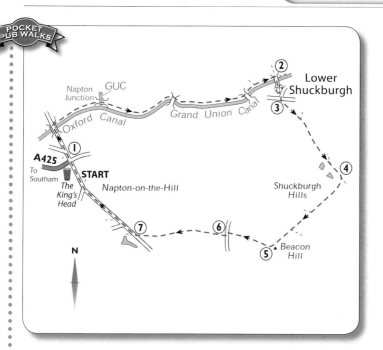

and then by the Grand Union Canal. The Oxford Canal was one of the first to be constructed in England and was built between 1769 and 1790 to carry goods and coal from the developing industrial areas in the Midlands to Oxford, and via the Thames to London. Royal assent was given in April 1769 and work began in Coventry in September. Financial problems meant it took nearly 20 years to reach Oxford and it was officially opened in 1790. A number of independent but connected waterways were formally combined in 1928 to form the 'Grand Union'. During the Second World War the canal was an important supply route to London and women ran the boats while the men were away. After the war, trade slipped away to road and rail transport, especially once the motorway network began to be built in the 1960s. But as trade declined the use of the canals for pleasure grew and this is now the main traffic.

[2] Leave the towpath and cross the bridge. Head towards a church seen ahead at **Lower Shuckburgh** and then on to reach a main road.

[3] Cross the road to a signed path, starting through a kissing-gate. Head half-left towards a farm. Go through two gates, then on in the same direction uphill, following the waymarks. Continue past a beacon and a small lake to find a more defined track leading to a kissing-gate by a field gate. Go through the gate and continue uphill in the same direction.

[4] As you approach the brow of the hill, take a fainter path leading right to a stile by a gate. Go over the stile to walk with a wood on the right to a stone trig point on **Beacon Hill**.

*The beacon.*

[5] From the trig point, bear right to a stile by a gate. Over the stile, turn right and head downhill to a pair of stiles in the bottom right-hand corner of the field, then carry on in the same direction to a lane.

[6] Turn left for 50 yards, then right through a small gate on a signed path. Head across a field, walking in the direction of **Napton**,

seen clustering around the hill ahead, to find a small gate and footbridge. Press on in the same direction towards **Napton**, navigating from stile to stile (some of which are rather awkward as they lack steps at the time of writing) to reach a double stile and footbridge giving on to a lane.

7 Turn right and walk along the lane to a T-junction, ignoring a lane on the left. Turn right to continue in the same direction to the **King's Head**.

## Places of interest nearby

The route does not pass through the main part of **Napton** but the walk can easily be extended to include a visit to this ancient village, by turning left along the lane passed in point 7. There has probably been a community here since before the Romans as it is such an excellent defensible site. By the Middle Ages it had become one of the largest towns in Warwickshire with about the same population of 1,000 people as it has today. For centuries two buildings have dominated the skyline of Napton village; high above the houses rise the outlines of the ancient church and the impressive windmill with its angular sails that are silhouetted against the sky. Seven counties are said to be visible from the top of this 500 ft hill on a fine day. The church of St Lawrence dates from the 12th century, was rebuilt in the 13th century and has later additions. As is often the case, there is a story that tells how the original church was to have been built near to the present village green. Each night, however, the stones that lay ready for its construction were transported by spirits to the summit of Napton hill. The villagers took the hint and the church was built on the hill overlooking the village nestling below. One wonders about the origin of these stories. Is it the legacy of an ancient village feud about where the church should be built?

# *The Green Dragon*

**T**his easy walk is very varied, with lanes, woods, field paths and a stretch by a pretty stream that might tempt you to linger – with a picnic, perhaps? It is an ideal walk to dawdle away a summer's afternoon with the promise of refreshment at the end. The first part along a country road is enlivened by some fine views and shaded by many noble trees, mainly oaks just coming into their prime. The route then leads through woodland, where bluebells give way to foxgloves as spring turns into summer. Another shady lane is followed by field paths that lead first by the stream then wend their way back to the village green at Sambourne, overlooked by the Green Dragon.

**Distance -** 4 miles.

**OS Explorer** 220 Birmingham. GR 060618.

Shady lanes, field paths and woods with no serious climbs.

**Starting point** The Green Dragon, Sambourne.

**How to get there** *Sambourne is signed from the B4090, Alcester to Droitwich road, 3 miles west of Alcester.*

**THE PUB**

The **Green Dragon** is a half-timbered building at the centre of this ancient hamlet, mentioned in the Domesday Book. The present building dates back to the second half of the 18th century and the landlords can be traced back to 1780. A plaque in the bar, presented by the Tony Hancock Society, commemorates the fact that the comedian's mother was licensee during the Second World War and he spent some of his leave from the RAF here. Possibilities for lunch range from sandwiches served on white, brown or ciabatta bread, served with soup if you wish. Omelettes and salads also feature, along with an extensive selection of full meals, including such interesting choices as breast of duck on bubble and squeak with port sauce.

*Food is served from 12 noon to 2 pm and from 6.30 pm in the evening*
☎ *01527 892465*

1. The **Green Dragon** lies at a crossroads in **Sambourne**. Take **Whitemoor Lane**, signed **'New End 1½ Droitwich 12'**. Walk along the road almost to its junction with the **B4090**, taking the left fork as you approach the junction.

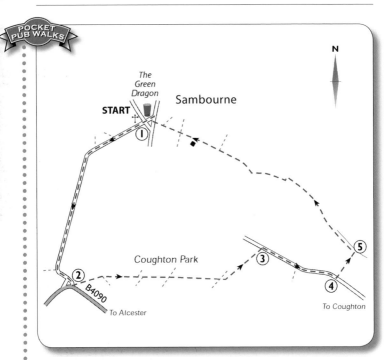

2 Turn left through a metal gate on a signed bridleway and follow the path across a field and into a wood. Just inside the wood, ignore a path on the right and press on in the same direction, ignoring all paths to left and right. At the end of the wood follow the path round to the left, now beside the wood, to a lane.

3 Turn right along the lane for about ¼ mile. Note the names of the buildings on the left – a clue as to what once passed near here.

4 Turn left along a fenced path starting through a metal kissing-gate beside a field gate. Carry on in the same direction across a field to a stream on the far side.

5 Turn left to walk beside the stream. When the way ahead is barred by a fence, bear left to a stile by a gate. Go ahead to another stile and then along the left-hand side of two fields. At the end of the second field, keep ahead on a wide grassy path along the right-hand side of a field. The path then leads past the farmyard of **Sambourne Hall**, going to the right of all buildings. Cross a

*The delightful village green at Sambourne.*

drive and press on in the same direction to find a stone stile onto a wide path that shortly leads to the village green and the **Green Dragon** in **Sambourne**.

## Places of interest nearby

The Throckmortons were an influential family in Tudor times and their country seat was **Coughton Court**, where they have lived from 1409 until the present. It is a National Trust property, though still managed by the Throckmortons, and open to the public on Wednesday to Sunday from the beginning of April to the end of September and at weekends in October between 11.30 am and 5 pm. The house is mainly Elizabethan, and was attacked by both Royalist and Parliamentary forces during the Civil War. It also had connections with the Gunpowder Plot. The Royal Horticultural Society has described the garden as 'stunning'. Coughton Court is on the A435, 2 miles north of Alcester.
☎ *01789 762435*

# The White Swan

**H**enley-in-Arden is an ancient market town and justly proud of its gracious mile-long High Street, lined with quaint old houses, shops of all kinds and, of course, several pubs. This walk starts by exploring part of it and then heads into the undulating countryside behind, climbing gently to one of the highest spots around. Where you have hills, you have views and this walk is no exception. The view today is probably better than it would have been hundreds of years ago when we would have been in the Forest of Arden. Today, there are fine vistas in all directions with the clue to the former nature of the landscape in the many majestic trees. The scenery could not be more English and the route joins the Heart of England Way to traverse many hay meadows, undoubtedly at their loveliest in early June before the vegetation is cut. The path leads to The Edge for another outstanding view and crosses the site of a Norman castle that once brooded over the town, before returning to Henley.

**THE PUB**

Directly opposite the church and Guildhall, the **White Swan** is one of Henley's old coaching inns and there has been an inn on the site since the 14th century. The low-ceiling, beamed and timbered bar is a popular meeting place, or you could sit outside. At lunchtime it serves a couple of specials such as, on my visit, smoked haddock with poached egg, if you have the appetite for a full meal. Lighter options include a range of sandwiches and a ploughman's. The traditional beers kept are Pedigree, Hooky bitter and Adnams' Broadside.

*Lunch is served between noon and 3 pm with sandwiches available all afternoon. Food is served in the evening from 6 pm onwards.*
☎ *01564 792623*

**Distance** 5 miles.

**OS Explorer** 220 Birmingham. GR 150659.

Easy walking on well signed field paths, tracks and quiet lanes.

**Starting point** Croft car park, Henley-in-Arden.

***How to get there*** *Henley-in-Arden is on the A3400, Stratford-upon-Avon to Birmingham road. The car park is signed from the High Street, the main road through the town.*

**1** From the car park, return to the **High Street** and turn left. Walk the length of the **High Street**, passing the **White Swan** on the left.

**2** Opposite the entrance to **Henley Golf Club**, turn right on a signed path that leads to a wooden kissing-gate into a field. Head across two fields towards some buildings seen ahead, to a field corner, then bear left to a metal kissing-gate. Through the gate turn right and follow the path over a stile to a lane.

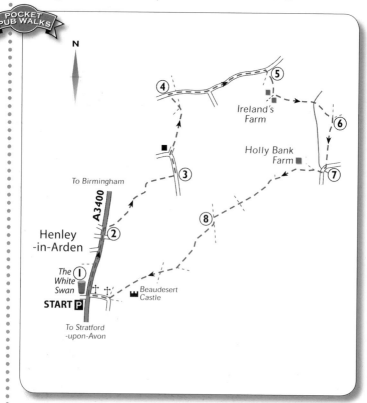

POCKET
PUB WALKS

N

④

⑤

Ireland's
Farm

⑥

Holly Bank
Farm

To Birmingham

A3400

③

⑦

⑧

Henley
-in-Arden

②

The ①
White
Swan

Beaudesert
Castle

START **P**

To Stratford
-upon-Avon

*The Henley Heritage Centre.*

**3** Turn left. At a junction by a house called **Laurels**, take the right fork. This soon becomes a track: continue along it to a lane.

**4** Turn right for a good ½ mile, ignoring a lane on the right.

**5** Turn right along a track, signed **'Ireland's Farm'**. Immediately before the farm, bear left on a smaller track that leads down into a valley and ends at a field gate. Carry on across a field to a bridge over a brook, then along the right-hand side of a field to a stile onto a cross-track, joining the **Heart of England Way**.

**6** Turn right and walk along the track to a lane.

**7** Turn right for 100 yards, then right again on a track towards **Holly Bank Farm** for 85 yards. Now bear left off the track to follow a waymarked path that leads first uphill past the farm, then from stile to stile across hay meadows to a track. Cross the track and keep on in the same direction, still on the **Heart of England Way**, to a T-junction with a cross-path.

**8** Turn left for 70 yards, then cross a stile on the right and head across a field to emerge on **The Edge**, which is a splendid viewpoint. Turn left to walk along **The Edge**, down into a dip and up the other side over the site of **Beaudesert Castle**, though there is little to see on the ground beyond a few suggestive humps. Press on down into **Henley** and go ahead along a road back to the **High Street**.

## Places of interest nearby

On the High Street at number 150 is **Henley Heritage Centre**, located in a 14th-century house and housing a collection recording a thousand years of the life of this small market town. The display about Beaudesert Castle and its excavation by BBC's *Time Team* in 2001 is particularly interesting. Admission to the Heritage Centre is free (though contributions are very welcome) and it is open Tuesday to Friday between 10.30 am and 4.30 pm.
☎ 01564 795919

Next door to the Heritage Centre is **Henley Ice Cream Parlour**, which sells a wide selection of their own delicious ice-creams. They are not quite so popular now as they were in the 1930s, when the trade brought chaos to Henley High Street and a uniformed man had to be employed to direct the traffic!

# 12 **Offchurch**

## *The Stag's Head*

**T**his interesting route has the most varied waterside walking of all those included in this book, with a substantial stretch by the Grand Union Canal, as well as by the River Leam and some ponds. It starts in Offchurch, which is situated on the side of a hill, with the charming thatched pub at the bottom and the ancient church at the top. It has many pretty cottages and extensive views over the surrounding countryside. A disused railway has been converted into a cycleway and so is easy walking with more views and an abundance of wild flowers and blackberries in season. This leads to the Grand Union Canal (see walk 9). Towpath walking is always easy and interesting with the antics of boaters as they navigate the locks providing added colour. Leaving the canal,

**Distance** - 5 miles.

**OS Explorer** 221 Coventry and Warwick. GR 359658.

One short climb out of Offchurch, followed by easy walking on cycleway and canal towpath. The return is on good paths through a nature reserve and parkland.

**Starting point** The Stag's Head, Offchurch.

*How to get there* *Offchurch is signed from the A425, about 2 miles east of Leamington Spa.*

the route then explores a nature reserve beside the River Leam before crossing attractive parkland back to Offchurch. This area is used for cross-country horse trials. When these are taking place the peace is somewhat disturbed by a commentary but this is more than compensated for by the entertainment value of watching the event, especially at the water jump.

**THE PUB** The **Stag's Head** at Offchurch is a picture-postcard country pub, complete with thatched roof. It is reputed to be haunted, though the present manager has never seen anything spooky. As well as the charming beamed bars, there are some tables outside in the garden. The excellent choice of food includes full meals and smaller versions of some are available for a lighter lunch. The beers include Deuchars IPA, Jennings and Adnams' Broadside, as well as guest ales.

*It serves food from noon until 2 pm during the week and until 2.30 pm at the weekend as well as in the evening, from 6 pm (6.30 pm at the weekend).*
☎ *01926 425801*

1. From the **Stag's Head** turn left up **School Hill**, signed **'Leamington 3¼'**. At the top of the hill, turn left at a T-junction, signed **'Long Itchington 3¾'**, to a second T-junction.

2. Cross the road to a stile, then follow the path ahead downhill. Immediately before a bridge, go through a gate on the right and walk down to a disused railway line. Turn right and follow this to a disused but still impressive bridge over the **Grand Union Canal**.

*A charming cottage in Offchurch.*

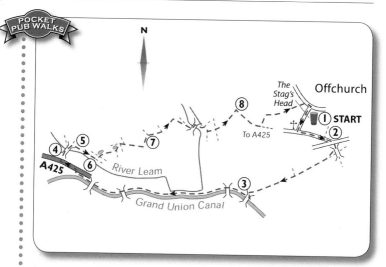

3 Turn right along the towpath. Some 230 yards after the third bridge, **number 36**, take some steps down on the right and turn left beside the main road, the **A425**, for 300 yards.

4 Turn right, signed **'Riverside Walk'**, through a small parking area, then follow the path over a bridge across the river and on for 90 yards.

5 Turn right on a smaller path to walk beside the **River Leam**.

6 Some 15 yards after a gate across the path, turn left away from the river. Shortly go over a cross path and continue ahead to reach a wooden barrier. Go through this into a field. Bear left to find a clear path and turn right along it. Ignore a clear path on the left, then follow the path round to the left to pass the end of a golf course.

7 When this path turns left, turn right across a field. At the far side, go across the end of a track, then bear left to walk along the left-

hand side of a field to a stile next to a field gate. The next part of the route is across parkland used for cross-country horse trials so there are many tracks and paths constructed in conjunction with this. Over the stile bear half right to find a footbridge over the **River Leam**. Cross the bridge and turn right to a second footbridge. Some 25 yards after this, turn right. Follow the path as it curves left and press on past some jumps and across a drive to reach a second drive.

⑧ Turn right. Immediately after a small lay-by on the right, turn left off the drive, shown by a yellow waymark arrow. Walk across an open area, then bear round to the right to find a stile on the left. Over the stile, go ahead to a stile by a gate onto a lane. Turn right back to the **Stag's Head** in **Offchurch**.

## Places of interest nearby

**Leamington Spa** grew from a small village into a major resort on the back of the craze in the early 19th century for taking the waters. The **Pump Rooms** were opened in 1814 to meet the needs of the ever-increasing number of visitors. Fashion moved on and the Pump Rooms were in a poor condition by the late 20th century. Fortunately, they have undergone a major refurbishment and are now home to the town's library and art gallery as well as a fascinating museum where there are displays on the historic use of the rooms and spa treatments, including several weird and wonderful objects from the former physiotherapy department. There is also the opportunity to sample spa water (for those who are brave enough!), reputed to cure all manner of ills and apparently a mild laxative. The building is open every day except Monday and Thursday mornings.
☎ 01926 742700

Across the road from the Pump Rooms are **Jephson Gardens**, also magnificently restored recently.

# The Raven

**T**his easy and more or less level walk makes an excellent half-day expedition. It starts in Brinklow, an ancient community on the Fosse Way that has been welcoming visitors since the Romans passed this way over 2,000 years ago. The longest stretch explores part of the Oxford Canal. I always enjoy canal walking: there are the boats to watch as they chug by, often with a friendly word, and the canal side is usually full of interest, with wild flowers, birds and insects to spot. To avoid the need for locks this canal, initially designed by the great canal engineer James Brindley, is first raised above the surrounding countryside and then channelled through a deep cutting clothed in trees. Originally, the canal wended through Brinklow itself but it was later straightened to bypass the village. The return to

**Distance -** 3½ miles.

**OS Explorer** 222 Rugby and Daventry. GR 435795.

Mainly canal towpath with some field paths and lanes.

**Starting point** The Raven, Brinklow.

*How to get there* *Brinklow is on the B4455, Fosse Way, and is signed from the A428, Coventry to Rugby road. The Raven is on the main road through the village.*

Brinklow crosses an unusually interesting field where some of the history of this community remains fossilised in the landscape.

**THE PUB** The **Raven** is a friendly village pub where you can be sure of a warm welcome. It is a Marston's house serving the full range of beers, together with a different guest beer every week. For a light lunch there are sandwiches or hot rolls filled with tasty bacon or sausage, as well as stuffed jacket potatoes. On a cold day the homemade soup is welcome and on my visit I found the hearty Scotch broth served by the Scottish landlady particularly sustaining. If you are feeling particularly hungry there is a choice of full meals such as steaks or a mixed grill. On Sunday just a full roast is served. There are some tables outside, with a children's play area.

*Food is served from 12.30 pm onwards*
☎ *01788 832655*

1 Turn left from the **Raven** for 40 yards, then right along **Barr Lane**. At the end of the lane, go ahead on a signed path that shortly leads into a field. Head diagonally across the field to find

a metal kissing-gate. Through the gate, turn right to walk along the right-hand side of three fields. At the end of the third field, bear right on a short path to a T-junction of paths.

**2** Turn right to a lane. Turn left for 75 yards, then turn right along a lane at a junction.

**3** Immediately before a bridge over the **Oxford Canal**, bear left down to the towpath and turn right by the canal. Walk beside the canal for 1¾ miles to the third bridge across the canal, numbered **34** on the far side from this direction. The bridge crossed on the

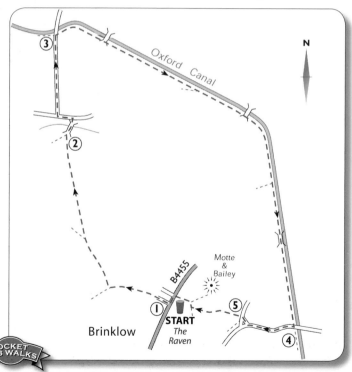

*The ancient village of Brinklow.*

towpath is where the canal used to turn into **Brinklow** but is impassable today.

4  Leave the canal up some steps and turn left along a road as far as its junction with **Eel Lane**, where the road turns sharp left.

5  At this point, carry on in the same direction on a waymarked path that leads to a stile after a few yards. Over the stile, go ahead across a field. In the next field, turn left to walk along the right-hand side of a field next to a wide ditch, part of the castle's defences. At the end of the field, bear right to a stile and cross-path. Turn left into **Brinklow** to emerge next to the **Raven**.

*The grassy mound of the castle is known locally as the Tump. Built on a natural rise, the hill and its associated earthworks are one of the best-preserved motte-and-bailey castle sites in the country. However, the name of Brinklow itself suggests a much older settled community, or at least a site that was important to people long before the Norman Conquest. The name is thought to originate from the personal name Brynca, and the word 'hlaw', meaning 'hill' in the sense of tumulus or burial mound. This ancient derivation implies that there was almost certainly a man-made 'tump' here long before the Normans exploited the site to build their castle in the 11th century after the Conquest. It was probably abandoned by the 13th century. Note also the pronounced ridges and furrows to the left, the remnants of the medieval farming system where local farmers drew lots to decide which ridge each would get to grow crops on every year.*

## Places of interest nearby

At **Ryton Organic Gardens**, ten acres of beautifully landscaped grounds highlight the delights of going organic. If you want to know how to turn your small back garden into a lush organic paradise with home-made compost, or just have a relaxing stroll to admire the beautiful flowers and shrubs, the 30 individually-themed gardens lure not only the keen gardener but offer plenty for the whole family. A new visitor centre tells the history of vegetables in the UK and has lots of interactive displays. You can also take a peep at the laboratories of the Heritage Seed Library, where rare vegetable varieties are saved and made available to gardeners. Did you know, for example, that there are 360 varieties of tomato in Britain? The gardens are open throughout the year between 9 am and 5 pm except during Christmas week and there is also a restaurant and teashop. The gardens are located 5 miles south-east of Coventry off the A45 and are amply signed. Despite the name they are not actually in Ryton-on-Dunsmore but on the outskirts of Wolston.

☎ 024 7630 3517

# 14 **Hartshill**

## *The Malt Shovel*

**T**his route packs an enormous variety into its 4 miles and so whatever sort of walking you enjoy, you are bound to find something to please you. It starts in Hartshill Green and soon leaves the village to climb through beautiful woods to a superb viewpoint, where your efforts are rewarded with extensive vistas across the surrounding countryside. More woodland walking and an open stretch over the brow of a hill with further views brings you to the Coventry Canal for a couple of miles of waterside walking. The towpath is very good so you can stride out here. Leaving the towpath, a country lane soon brings you back to Hartshill Green.

The woods and open hillside are part of Hartshill Hayes Country Park. If you wish to call in at Hartshill Green for lunch part way round the walk, the route works very well starting at the country park car park (charge), which is signed locally. In this case, take the surfaced path behind the visitor centre to pick up the route at point 3.

**THE PUB** The **Malt Shovel** in Hartshill Green serves an exceptionally extensive menu ranging from sandwiches through salads and omelettes to full meals, including daily specials written on the blackboard. Vegetarians are unusually well served with interesting options such as butternut ginger bake, which is butternut squash and spinach in a tomato and ginger sauce. This is complemented by a tempting range of traditional puddings such as spotted dick. A free house, the beers include Banks's Original and Mild, Marston's Pedigree and Burton and Mansfield. There are some tables outside at the front and in a pretty courtyard at the rear.

*Food is served all day from noon throughout the week.*
☎ *024 7639 2501*

**Distance -** 4 miles.

**OS Explorer** 232 Nuneaton and Tamworth. GR 327946.

Woods, open hillside and canal towpath.

**Starting point** The Malt Shovel, Grange Road, Hartshill Green.

***How to get there*** *Hartshill is signed from the A5 about 2 miles east of Atherstone. Approaching Hartshill Green from the A5 along the main road through the village, turn left at the village green and take the first left, Grange Road, to the Malt Shovel on the left.*

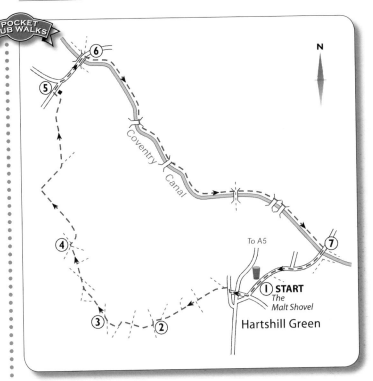

1 Turn right along the road from the **Malt Shovel**. At a T-junction bear right to the main road. Cross the road and note the blue plaque on the block of flats that now stands on the site of the cottage where Hartshill's most famous son, **Michael Drayton**, was born. At the end of the block of flats, turn left on a signed path. Do **not** go through a gate on the right but stay on the left side of the fence and follow the path down some steps, across a long footbridge over a boggy area and up the other side. Stay on the main path through the woods, ignoring all side paths, to a prominent cross-path marked by numbered posts on the right.

*Michael Drayton was a 16th-century poet. He was educated in the*

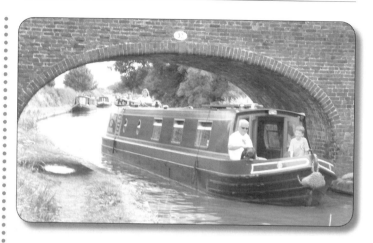

*The Coventry Canal.*

*household of Sir Henry Goodere at Polesworth (see walk 15). Little is known of his life, though we do know from his copious writings that he loved the Warwickshire countryside and was besotted with his patron's daughter, Anne. He continued to visit her after she was married and living at Clifford Chambers, south of Stratford-upon-Avon. He was able to eke out a living in London and, as one of the circle of poets and playwrights of the time, almost certainly knew Shakespeare (see walk 6). His fortunes declined towards the end of his life but he had the distinction of being buried in Westminster Abbey where there is a monument to him.*

**2** Turn left for 25 yards, then right to continue uphill. Keep ahead uphill at a cross-path. At the top of the hill, within sight of the **Hartshill Hayes Country Park** car park, bear right to reach a surfaced path.

**3** Turn right. When the path forks, take the left option to stay on the upper path. Keep ahead as a path joins on the left, and follow the path as it goes downhill, ignoring all others to right and left.

**4** Eventually the path turns sharp right and crosses a footbridge. Over the bridge, follow the path round the right-hand perimeter of a field and stay on it as it jinks to the other side of the hedge and continues in the same direction. At the end of the field, press on along the path as it turns right and climbs over the brow of a hill and then descends the other side, ignoring a path branching right, to eventually pass by a farmyard to reach a lane.

**5** Turn right, then right again at a T-junction to a bridge over the **Coventry Canal**.

*The Coventry Canal runs from Fradley near Lichfield to Coventry city centre and was built to transport coal from the pits at Bedworth, Coventry and Nuneaton throughout the Midlands and beyond. The Act of Parliament that allowed the canal to be built was passed in 1768. The great James Brindley was appointed as the engineer and work soon began building the canal in both directions from Longford, near Coventry. It was opened through to Atherstone in 1771 but then work slowed and the canal was not completed until 1790. Its main use was in the transport of stone and coal, but, in the early 1820s the canal was also used to carry soldiers. Eventually it began to suffer from competition from the railways, although it clung on longer than most canals and was used commercially until the 1970s.*

**6** Go over the bridge and turn right down to the canal. Turn left along the towpath as far as **bridge 30**, the sixth bridge.

**7** Leave the canal and go up to a lane. Turn left along the lane and follow it into **Hartshill Green**, where it becomes **Grange Road** and passes the **Malt Shovel**.

*Pretty Pigs*

**A** walk round a disused coal mine might not sound very attractive but don't let that put you off! This route is full of interest, both human and natural. The mine opened in 1846 and produced coal until 1965. The colliery was the first in the country to generate its own electricity from surplus steam and the first to have pithead baths. After the mine closed, the site lay derelict for many years until it was acquired by Warwickshire County Council and it is now managed as a country park. It is fascinating to see how natural processes are healing the scars left by mining and this is a particularly interesting walk if you are keen on birds. A Heritage Centre, open at the weekends at the time of writing (telephone 01827 897438, free) recalls the hard lives of the miners. In addition, it has a café with an attractive

# Pooley Fields & Alvecote Walk 15

patio overlooking the canal for refreshment part way round the walk. The route also passes close to the site of Alvecote Priory and there is a pleasant stretch by the Coventry Canal leading into Polesworth. All in all, this walk is both attractive and interesting and you should allow plenty of time to enjoy all it has to offer.

**THE PUB**
Housed in a former manor house a very short way into Staffordshire, **Pretty Pigs** is an exceptionally popular pub, hence the huge car park opposite. The food is exceptional value for money with a very reasonably-priced carvery as the centrepiece. If your appetite isn't up to generous slices of roast with all the trimmings, then something from the starter menu or a choice of salads makes a lighter lunch. Pretty Pigs also serves filled baguettes with, unusually, a serving of roasties. Traditional puds such as treacle sponge or apple and blackberry pie fill up any empty corner. The beers include Bass, Tetley and John Smith's. There are extensive gardens at the rear overlooking some of Alvecote Pools.

*Food is served between noon and 2 pm and from 6 pm.*
☎ *01827 63129.*

**Distance -** 5½ miles.

**OS Explorer** 232 Nuneaton and Tamworth. GR 239047.

Canal towpath and paths in country park, with some road walking.

**Starting point** The Pretty Pigs pub, Alvecote.

**How to get there** *Pretty Pigs is on the road to Shuttington on the north-east edge of Tamworth.*

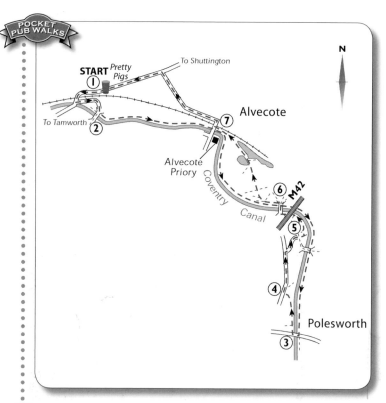

1 Turn left out of the **Pretty Pigs'** car park (right out of the pub) and walk along the road. Cross the bridge over the railway. Take the first turning on the left, before the canal and almost back on yourself, and walk to the end of the road. Go ahead on a path a few yards to a bridge over the **Coventry Canal** (see walk 14), then turn right down to the towpath.

2 Turn left along the towpath and walk beside the canal as far as **Polesworth**.

**3** Leave the towpath and turn right over the canal. Almost immediately, turn right again on an unsigned surfaced path. Continue ahead just inside a belt of trees when the surface shortly ends. When the path leaves the trees, carry on in the same direction round the right perimeter of the field to a lane.

**4** Turn right to walk along the lane, bearing right at a fork, signed **'Pooley Fields Heritage Centre'**. At the end of the tarmac, carry on along the main track, bearing slightly left to the **Heritage Centre**.

**5** Opposite the **Heritage Centre**, turn left up into a car park. Turn right round the car park until you come to a broad path on the right. Turn right along it and walk down, under the **M42**, to cross a footbridge over the canal to reach two gates with kissing-gates beside them.

*The route passes close to Alvecote Priory.*

# Warwickshire

**6** Go through the gate on the left and follow the broad path ahead, passing an information board. Follow this path until it eventually rejoins the canal and reaches a lane.

*The mound on the right is a former waste tip that is gradually being clothed in vegetation. You can nip up to the top, if you wish, for the view and to look for fossils.*

**7** Turn right along the lane and walk through **Alvecote** to a T-junction. Turn left back to the **Pretty Pigs**.

## Places of interest nearby

The ruins of **Alvecote Priory** can be seen across the canal. To visit the site, at point 7, turn left along the lane for 200 yards. It was founded in 1159 by William Burdet, who gave all the land he owned in Shuttington and Alvecote, including the mill, to support it. There is a local tradition that it was out of remorse for murdering his wife, because he suspected her of infidelity, only afterwards to find his suspicions unfounded. More likely he was 'persuaded' by his feudal overlord, Robert Beaumont Earl of Leicester.

**Polesworth** is said to be the last resting place of the great Queen Boudicca after her defeat by the Roman legions in AD 60. The abbey, in particular, is well worth visiting. It was founded in the 9th century by King Egbert and prospered for many centuries. It is close to the centre of the town and is well signed. You could visit it part way round the walk by turning left as you leave the canal at point 3 and following the signs. The medieval abbey gateway still stands to the west of the church, which became the parish church of St Editha. A beautiful and peaceful sensory garden has recently been built on the site of the former cloisters. The abbey and garden are open to visitors every day between 10 am and noon and 2 to 4 pm.
☎ *01827 892340*